Winning at Facebook Marketing with Zero Budget

Optimise your Page and posts for maximum organic reach without paying for ads:

A guide to cracking Facebook's 'Edgerank' Algorithm for your Page and your content

MARIE PAGE

DIGITERATI
Academy

Winning at Facebook Marketing with Zero Budget

Intro

Only a tiny minority of your fans actually see the content you put on Facebook. Some research puts this as low as 2%.

Using a complex algorithm, taking into account some 100,000 factors, Facebook suppresses your content so only very few of your intended audience sees it unless you pay to "boost" your posts.

This guide is intended to reveal the main workings of the algorithm and show you how you can use that knowledge to improve your reach and engagement organically. Without paying for ads.

With multiple examples, we cover the best types of content to use on Facebook, how to present it for maximum reach, how to avoid being unwittingly penalised by the algorithm, and share the tips and tricks you need to know to use this channel successfully.

An accompanying online course is available at **www.digiterati-academy.com**

The guide is intended for you to dip in and out of and is structured logically for optimum learning:

Part 1 – Are your fans beyond your reach?

Part 2 – Reach 101: Getting the basics right

Part 3 – How to influence your reach by what and how you post

Part 4 – Avoiding reach killers

Part 5 – Other factors, tricks and tips

Part 6 – Other ways of beating the algorithm

Part 7 – Summary of learning

About The Digiterati

The Digiterati is a collective of leading digital marketing experts. We care deeply about – and deliver against – our clients' business and marketing challenges.

After examining your needs, problems and objectives we develop highly tailored digital marketing solutions – taking into consideration every relevant discipline or channel – specific to your market, business and its level of digital maturity.

Our solutions range from extensive digital marketing strategies to tactical 'done for you' services, from company-wide training to one-to-one coaching. Crucially, we are different because, wherever possible, we strive to build your own digital capability within your business, making you less reliant on third parties.

We help businesses of all sizes from the world's leading multinational brands to 'solopreneur' micro-businesses. Our attention to detail and passion for delivering solid results is consistent irrespective of size, status or budget.

Our origins

Our team came together over a three-year period on what is considered the world's most impressive Digital Marketing MSc, delivered by Manchester Metropolitan Business School (a top 5% global business school[1]) in partnership with leading digital marketing publisher Econsultancy. During this time we came to realise we were very much among the elite of digital marketers worldwide – and coined the term Digiterati to describe ourselves. We began to collaborate on projects at an early stage – bringing in our peers for projects, client work and more.

1. Source: AACSB via http://www.mmu.ac.uk/news/news-items/4138/

Quite early on we identified that the majority of businesses are still in the very early stages of digital maturity and totally baffled by the multitude of possible digital marketing options. They didn't know what to begin with and had nowhere to turn for impartial advice. When asked they told us they seldom knew which providers or agencies to trust, which to work with or what they were paying for.

These businesses were frustrated at the lack of experience, strategic thinking and general digital know-how of their existing agencies. Many of these agencies, themselves struggling with digital transformation, would never turn away digital marketing work despite only having surface knowledge of it. So we found ourselves picking up the pieces of projects that had been poorly advised and implemented, with clients wishing they had found us at the project's inception.

The Digiterati was born in 2014 to address all these pain-points and become a trusted source of digital excellence. Since then, through training, consultancy, publications and our online activities we have helped thousands of businesses of all sizes and market sectors in the UK, US and Europe.

Our mantra is *relentless pursuit of digital excellence.*

Together we will help you achieve it.

Contents

Part 1 – Are your fans beyond your reach?

The truth about reach

There was a time when the adage "If you build it, they will come" was relatively true for brands taking their first steps onto Facebook. There was no advertising, there were fewer brands with Pages, and there was a lot less competition on the news feed (there are now 18 million brands clamouring for user attention). It wasn't hard to post something and get it seen by an extraordinarily high proportion of your fan base.

The concept that all your fans are guaranteed to see all your content has never been the case, but in recent years the visibility of content to fans has dropped further and further. This level of visibility is known as "Reach" of which there are three types:

- **Organic reach** – the number of your fans that see your posts in their news feed without you as the Page paying for any promotion such as a "boost".

- **Paid reach** – the number of people (which depending on your targeting may or may not be fans) that see your posts as a result of you paying for extra visibility.

- **Viral reach** – the number of non fans that see your posts as a result of their friends sharing, liking or commenting on your content with that "reaction" appearing on friends of fans timelines.

Of course not everyone with a Facebook profile is regularly using it. That will account for some of your lack of visibility: simply put, those people are not looking. Sometimes profiles are created then abandoned, or not memorialised when someone dies. And indeed there are numerous fake profiles that have been created by dodgy practitioners who made a living selling fake fans to brands interested in artificially increasing their vanity metrics.

It came as a shock to Page admins when Facebook first started seriously throttling reach. "Only 30% of our fans are seeing our content – that's outrageous" you'd hear marketing managers complain. Nowadays most Admins would be pretty happy with 30% organic reach.

The truth is that despite you having worked really hard to build a fan base, hardly any of them will actually see a thing you post. Reach has been dropping like a stone for some time.

Take a look at this Ogilvy research from Feb 2014 finding reporting average organic reach as low as 6%, and for large pages (with more than 500,000 fans) a little over 2%.

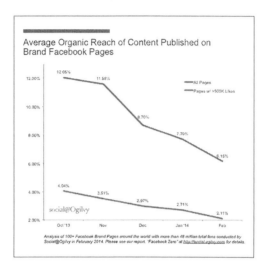

A more recent 2015 Locowise study, this time of 5,000 Pages (the Ogilvy research was of 100+ Pages), paints a similarly dismal picture:

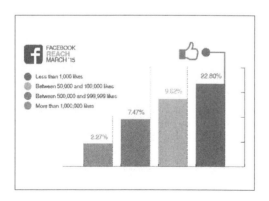

What is immediately apparent from the Locowise research is how Facebook appears to treat Pages differently according to how many fans (Likes) they have. That's bad news for you if, in the past, you've bought fans unwisely for an impressive looking KPI. At The Digiterati we have always said that total fan numbers is a vanity metric. We were quoting the following even when reach was good:

"Fans are vanity. Reach and Engagement is sanity."

This adage still holds true. Reach is nigh on impossible without engagement, engagement is impossible without reach (or at least a decent budget to force content into news feed).

This relationship between reach and engagement is at the heart of why and how Facebook decides what to show in your news feed. Engagement may come in the form of a click, a like, a comment or a share.

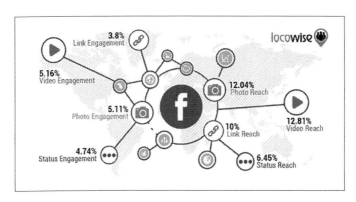

Locowise[2] repeats its research regularly and it's March 2016 findings paint a slightly more positive picture with average Page reach of 11.41% of fans. This breaks down as follows:

- Video: 12.81%
- Photos: 12.04%
- Links: 10.00%
- Status Updates: 6.45%

2. http://locowise.com/blog/facebook-page-reach-up-by-60-percent-since-november-2015

Be aware that no single study of average reach is going to be 100% accurate, and any Page Admin that keeps a keen eye on their metrics will know that reach can fluctuate from month to month. Facebook doesn't generally publish global reach figures, so any commercial study is simply looking at a small sample of Pages.

The Locowise research is the highest average reach figure that we've seen in several years of studies. This study is from Locowise client Pages, namely brands that invest in Facebook on multiple levels. Brands that are going to be doing a lot right to optimise their reach. So we can conclude that 11.4% reach is on the optimal front as a target for other Pages to reach. Sure you'll get the odd post that does a lot better, but an awful lot of your content will have simply dismal reach figures.

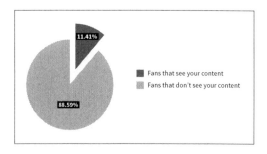

Facebook has over a billion daily active users. Even back in 2013[3] it was quoted as saying that there are on average 1,500 potential stories from friends, people you follow and Pages that you could see each day. At the time, Facebook announced one of many algorithm updates that enabled them to prioritise about 300 of these stories to appear in your newsfeed. Since then, with many more users and many more Pages in existence, news feed pressure has only increased.

50 million businesses now use Facebook Pages. And over a billion of Facebook's users are connected to at least one business Page: in the US, that's over 80% of users.

3. https://www.facebook.com/business/news/News-Feed-FYI-A-Window-Into-News-Feed

Facebook now has 3 million active advertisers[4] with 500,000 new advertisers being added every six months.

The platform has also put huge emphasis into monetisation for its shareholders so has become more "pay to play" for brands than ever before. See this assessment of Facebook's falling reach alongside its rising stock price from Jay Baer[5].

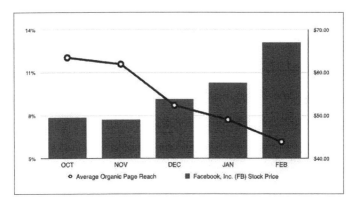

An insightful article[6] in the January 2016 edition of The Slate by senior technology writer Will Oremus, confirmed that an ever more sophisticated algorithm is at work. Oremus went to Facebook's news feed team at their California headquarters to learn more.

He discovered that whilst the average Facebook user could easily see over 1,500 posts per day in an unfiltered news feed, those with a few hundred friends could have as many as 10,000 stories vying for their attention. Most of us would simply turn off if that much data was being thrown at us every time we glanced at our phones.

4. http://locowise.com/blog/facebook-page-reach-up-by-60-percent-since-november-2015
5. http://www.convinceandconvert.com/social-media-tools/this-chart-explains-the-reachpocalypse-and-why-facebook-is-laughing-all-the-way-to-the-bank/
6. http://www.slate.com/articles/technology/cover_story/2016/01/how_facebook_s_news_feed_algorithm_works.html

The problem was explained in an article[7] published in Facebook's Newsroom in June 2016:

"When we launched News Feed in 2006, it was hard to imagine the challenge we now face: far too much information for any one person to consume. In the decade since, more than a billion people have joined Facebook, and today they share a flood of stories every day. That's why stories in News Feed are ranked — so that people can see what they care about first, and don't miss important stuff from their friends. If the ranking is off, people don't engage, and leave dissatisfied. So one of our most important jobs is getting this ranking right."

Google's algorithm

Search engine Google operates an algorithm called PageRank to decide what to show you at the top of its search results. Websites vie to be number 1 on Google, sitting at the very top of the first page. You may well have been aware of some major updates made to this algorithm, such as the updates named Panda, Pigeon, Penguin and more. Search Engine Optimisation (SEO) is a method of optimising your website to get as high up in Google results as possible. PageRank determines what to show a user based on a search by key word or key phrase. As well as factors such as the number of quality links going to the website of choice, it also adds a layer (coined the "Filter Bubble[8]") which factors in your personal search and click history in order to deliver results more personalised to your history, interests and preferences.

Facebook's algorithm is similar. It brings together tens of thousands of factors that are both to do with possible Posts and Pages and type of content as well as what it already knows about your preferences and behaviours.

In the past, Facebook's algorithm was known as "Edgerank"[9] (adapting Google's PageRank name and replacing Page with Edge – Facebook's then term for any individual piece of content).

---

7. http://newsroom.fb.com/news/2016/06/building-a-better-news-feed-for-you/
8. The Filter Bubble: What the Internet is Hiding From You, by Eli Pariser, 2011
9. http://marketingland.com/edgerank-is-dead-facebooks-news-feed-algorithm-now-has-close-to-100k-weight-factors-55908

The algorithm has not been referred to internally at Facebook as Edgerank for some years now and they now refer to content "Edges" as "Stories".

You can watch Adam Mosseri, VP of Product Management for News Feed talking at F8, 2016 about how the algorithm works in broad terms here:

http://newsroom.fb.com/news/2016/04/news-feed-fyi-from-f8-how-news-feed-works/

Mosseri says:

"The goal of News Feed is to show people the stories that matter most to them, whether it's from friends or Pages. Our role on News Feed is to connect people with the stories that matter to them most."

A 2013 announcement by Lars Backstrom, Director of Engineering at Facebook stated:

"The goal of News Feed is to deliver the right content to the right people at the right time so they don't miss the stories that are important to them. Ideally, we want News Feed to show all the posts people want to see in the order they want to read them."[10]

The principles used today in ranking each story that appears in your timeline is, according to Mosseri, as follows:

- How likely are you to 'Like' the story?
- To share the story?
- To spend time on the story?

Facebook's algorithm considers who posted the story and how connected you are to them, how others are interacting with the post – is it getting lots of Likes, Reactions, Comments or Shares? And are any of those from people that you know too? It'll consider the type of content – if you like watching videos but tend to ignore links, it's more likely to show you videos than links. It also considers how recent the story was – recent updates normally the most relevant.

---

10. https://www.facebook.com/business/news/News-Feed-FYI-A-Window-Into-News-Feed

Here's an example from Mosseri from his own news feed that he shared at F8 in 2016. The annotations show some of the factors that Facebook takes into account when deciding what to show:

Facebook also considers a bunch of factors that potentially override the recency monitor and will show older stories that it considers particularly relevant to the user (an announcement of a close friend's engagement posted the previous day may well be shown higher in the news feed than a very recent photo of an acquaintance's breakfast).

All the above factors give each story a "Relevancy Score". Stories may come from your friends, people you follow or brands (Pages) that you like (we're going to ignore the part that ads play in the news feed for the time being). For any single user, the relevance score of each story is very specific to them, akin to Google's filter bubble.

On Facebook each story is given a score and then ordered on your time line with the stories Facebook feels are the most relevant at the top. Another Mosseri screen grab:

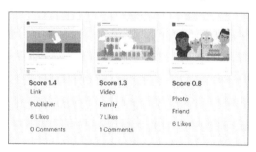

When you come back to Facebook an hour or so later the process repeats itself with all the new content that is now available to you.

How does Facebook know what is relevant to you?

Facebook is sitting on a cyber mountain of data about your click history, your friendship circles, your stated preferences, your Likes and way, way more (that's one of the reasons targeting for Facebook advertisers can be so awesome).

But it doesn't just rely on click data, it has a Feed Quality Panel comprised of users who are asked to organise their stories in order of preference. It also carries out regular online surveys – you may even have been asked to take part in this (it's happened to me a number of times) and seen something like the following:

What are the thousands of factors in this algorithm?

In determining which stories Facebook thinks are most relevant for you, it takes on board around 100,000 factors.

Based on what I've read from Facebook, other creditable sources as well as what I've observed through experimentation with multiple Pages over the years, I've created the following simplified equation of how the algorithm, or relevancy score, works.

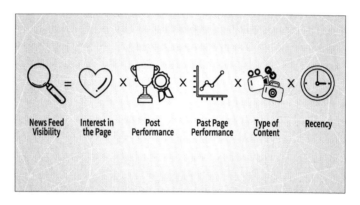

- **News Feed Visibility (often described as "Σ" for "EdgeRank")** – this is based on a score of how relevant Facebook considers the story to be and takes into account a wide number of factors. A story can be a status update, photo, video, comment, like, tag, event, relationship status change or any of the other pieces of content that you see in news feed.

- **Interest** – this is concerned with how interested you are in the creator of the story. Is it a best friend you engage with all the time on Facebook, a mere acquaintance you barely interact with, a brand you love and share content from regularly or a brand you've lost interest in and ignored in recent times. Interest is also known as "affinity" and is gauged by how long you spent in the past on stories that person/Page has posted, how you reacted to those stories (clicked, liked, commented, shared etc).

- **Post Performance** – this considers how well this story is performing with other users and the kind of reactions it is getting.

- **Past Page Performance** – this element concerns the standing of the Page - is it verified? What type of Page is it? Does it have complete profile information? How old is it? How many fans does it have? How engaged are those fans with the Page and its recent content?

- **Type/Weight** – there are two overarching factors at play here. Facebook itself weights some types of post more highly than others (in 2016 it prefers natively uploaded Facebook video[11] above anything else). It also factors in the type of content a user prefers – do they look at lots of photos on Facebook, click a lot of links, watch videos regularly? So some content types are given a higher score and promoted, and less popular types of content will get a lower reach and either sit lower in the news feed or barely be shown at all.

- **Recency** – this is to do with the age of a post. Generally the longer a story has been live the less likely it is to be seen. There will be exceptions: with personal posts, announcements of, for example, engagements, tend to stick around news feed for longer. And for Page posts, "Story Bumping" kicks in when an older story suddenly starts to get a lot of interactions.

The algorithms at work

It should be becoming clear from the above that there are two basic algorithms at work on Facebook for organic updates. These decide:

- What stories to show you
- What order those stories are shown in

This book is not about Facebook ads, but it is worth reflecting that an algorithm is also at work deciding which ads to show you. This is affected by:

- The relevance score – how relevant is this ad to you based on your interests and past click history?
- The amount of text in the ad – ads with a lot of text are discouraged by Facebook
- The price paid – the higher the price, the more visibility

---

11. http://www.adweek.com/socialtimes/quintly-native-videos-study/631812

- The reputation of the advertiser
- The reaction of other users to seeing the ad
- The competition for your news feed from other advertisers
- And much more

Friends and family come first

In June 2016 an announcement[12] to an algorithm change was made that prioritises posts from your friends and family:

"If it's from your friends, it's in your feed, period — you just have to scroll down."

Furthermore these updates are towards the top of the news feed.

The announcement also gave further insight into the thinking behind the algorithm:

Our research has also shown us that, after friends and family, people have two other strong expectations when they come to News Feed:

Your feed should inform. *People expect the stories in their feed to be meaningful to them — and we have learned over time that people value stories that they consider informative. Something that one person finds informative or interesting may be different from what another person finds informative or interesting — this could be a post about a current event, a story about your favorite celebrity, a piece of local news, or a recipe. We're always working to better understand what is interesting and informative to you personally, so those stories appear higher up in your feed.*

Your feed should entertain. *We've also found that people enjoy their feeds as a source of entertainment. For some people, that's following a celebrity or athlete; for others it's watching Live videos and sharing funny photos with their friends. We work hard to try to understand and predict what posts on Facebook you find entertaining to make sure you don't miss out on those.*

---

12. http://newsroom.fb.com/news/2016/06/building-a-better-news-feed-for-you/

Making the newsfeed "informative"

In August 2016 Facebook made an announcement that it was tweaking the newsfeed to show more "personally informative stories"[13]. Emphasising that what you will want to see in your feed is uniquely personal a press release stated:

"Something that one person finds informative may be different from what another person finds informative. This could be a news article on a current event, a story about your favorite celebrity, a piece of local news, a review of an upcoming movie, a recipe or anything that informs you."

Understanding those personal preferences is undertaken in part by Facebook's Feed Quality Program that we looked at in Part 1 – a global crowd-coursed survey of tens of thousands of people per day who answer detailed questions about what they like to see. A key factor is whether the story helps inform people of the world around them.

The clue to how this is determined is held in the explanation:

"Generally, we've found people find stories informative if they are related to their interests, if they engage people in broader discussions and if they contain news about the world around them."

So a story that chimes with known interests, that is engaging people in online conversation and is newsworthy is more likely to be seen. And as usual factors such as your relationship with the person or publisher that posted, the content type and your propensity to engage with it helps the algorithm predict stories that you might personally find informative.

---

13. http://newsroom.fb.com/news/2016/08/news-feed-fyi-showing-you-more-personally-informative-stories/

Story bumping

Back in September 2013, in a rare announcement in relation to an algorithm tweak, Facebook introduced Story Bumping. The Story Bump shows you posts you may not have seen when they were first published.

As we've seen, your news feed is normally full of relatively recent stories. But occasionally you may see something much older. The post below surfaced for me 24 hours after it was published:

Similarly this post was 8 hours old:

In tests, Facebook found that the Story Bump resulted in an 8% increase in likes, comments and shares so it has remained in news feed, albeit not quite as aggressively as when it was first launched.

A study by Wisemetrics[14] at the time Story Bumping was announced showed that it only takes 2 hours and 30 minutes for a post to get 75% of its total impressions and less than 2 hours to get 75% of its maximum reach.

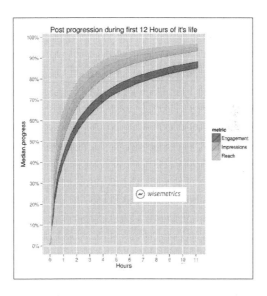

Story Bumping pops your post back into the news feed if it is getting good engagement. One way I have found of influencing this is by sending an email out that contains a link to that post.

14. http://www.wiselytics.com/blog/facebook-posts-lifetime-even-shorter-than-you-thought/

Last actor

Facebook tracks your last 50 interactions on a rolling basis and uses these as additional signals to rank your feed. This keeps your personal algorithm factors very up-to-date and also explains why you see posts from newly liked Pages very quickly in news feed.

An important caveat

Before you read any further I want to make a number of things clear:

- I don't work and have never worked for Facebook

- I don't have any insider knowledge of Facebook's working beyond what is already in the public domain. Instead I have many years experience of running successful Facebook Pages that consistently outperform others for reach and engagement. I have also researched the topic extensively for years and even have a First Class Masters Degree with a Facebook research specialism.

So what you are reading in this book is a combination of facts as stated by Facebook themselves (these are all in the public domain and can be found via research on Google), commonly accepted best practices for optimal reach (as agreed by multiple Facebook experts – again all Googleable) and my own research and observations of what works well on multiple Facebook Pages as well as those of my Digiterati colleagues and our clients. What I've not seen in other publications is all these many sources pulled together in a single book or paper that has the sole focus of investigating the Facebook algorithm.

Of course the algorithm changes frequently, so factors that were identified in the past may not now work in the same way. I've therefore selected those factors that I either know, or observe to still be relevant at the time of writing.

It is very possible that some of the factors I've identified won't work for you. Or don't work for you with the content you have posted, at the time you have posted it, on the Page you've posted it and with that fan base. As Facebook's VP of Product Management says: go and try things.

Read this book, take the accompanying online course (www.digiterati-academy.com) and put it into practice. See what works for your Page, for your audience. Take some of my ideas and try them out. Adapt them. Let me know what you find.

The algorithm is constantly being updated. And whilst the majority of the principles I've listed here are with us for the long term, change is inevitable.

For updates go to The Digiterati's blog (www.thedigiterati.com/blog) or our Facebook Page (www.facebook.com/teamdigiterati) where we publish all our latest findings, observations and research. We'd also love to have you join our Facebook Group (www.facebook.com/groups/teamdigiterati).

Optimising your Page for visibility in Google

This book isn't really about SEO of your Facebook content on Google, it's about the visibility of your content within Facebook itself.

Having said that it is worth understanding the basic things you can do to improve your Page's ranking on Google. Many of these have resonance with SEO good practice for a website.

1. Choose a Facebook name with appropriate keywords

That's easier said than done but clearly your brand name is a good place to start along with the kind of search keywords people are using to find your website or Page. The first word in a multi-word title will get the most weight from Google and be seen as the most important.

2. Create a username (vanity url) that reflects your brand and key words

You can search for user name availability here https://www.facebook.com/username

3. Use your keywords

As with conventional SEO on websites, keywords are crucial so use them in the important areas of your Page such as your About information, Mission and Company description. See below how the Short Description surfaces in the Google SERP results:

Short Description   Supercharge your social media. Optimise your online presence. Get advice & support that delivers results.

Google SERP result for search for "The Digiterati Facebook"

The Digiterati | Facebook
https://www.**facebook**.com/Team**Digiterati**/ ▾
The Digiterati. 672 likes · 30 talking about this. Supercharge your social media. Optimise your online presence. Get advice & support that delivers results.

4. Fill in all the detail on your profile

You'd be surprised at how many Pages have incomplete About info. Not only does Facebook itself view that dimly, but Google places higher important on Pages that have information such as phone numbers and addresses.

5. Work your back links

As with conventional SEO, back links are important. Make sure you have links to your Facebook Page from your website and other social media platforms like LinkedIn and Twitter.

6. Optimise status updates

Think about keyword usage in your posts – the first 18 characters serve as the meta title and meta description in the SERP on Google and remember that Google considers the first word more important than the second.

7. Use Facebook Notes

Facebook Notes have been around for a very long time but few Pages use them. They can and do index well on Google though. Again think about utilising key search words in the title of the note. With the new Page layout from Summer 2016 it is possible to display Notes quite prominently in the right hand column[15].

Google and Facebook are not exactly the best of friends. They are competing for your online time. Google's algorithms will not be keen to index much of what is happening on Facebook and its search spiders seem to crawl Facebook Pages and index their content a lot less regularly than they do websites. This means your Facebook stories aren't often found in Google's results page.

Identifying the reach you currently have

Firstly, Facebook's reach figures can be misleading. Take this post by Musicademy (which is a Page I've built from scratch). At the point this screen grab was taken the Page had 14,364 fans. It's a neat case study looking at multiple factors that optimise a post for reach.

The post below achieved a reach of 11,017. I know – you must be thinking, "Wow – this girl really knows her stuff – that's reach of 77%! Surely that's unheard of nowadays."

---

15. https://thedigiterati.com/new-facebook-page-design-re-order-columns/

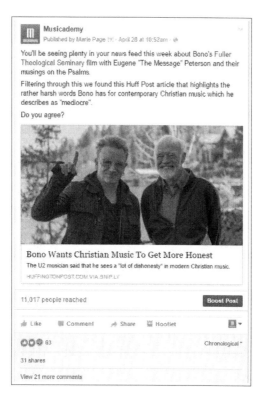

Musicademy
Published by Marie Page [?] · April 28 at 10:52am · @

You'll be seeing plenty in your news feed this week about Bono's Fuller Theological Seminary film with Eugene "The Message" Peterson and their musings on the Psalms.

Filtering through this we found this Huff Post article that highlights the rather harsh words Bono has for contemporary Christian music which he describes as "mediocre".

Do you agree?

Bono Wants Christian Music To Get More Honest
The U2 musician said that he sees a "lot of dishonesty" in modern Christian music.
HUFFINGTONPOST.COM VIA .SNIP.LY

11,017 people reached   Boost Post

👍 Like   💬 Comment   ↗ Share   Hootset   ▾

○○○ 63   Chronological ▾

31 shares

View 21 more comments

Well it is pretty unusual, but it is possible, especially for really hot content and particularly with what I'd describe as a passion brand sharing content about a topic their fans are passionate about.

There are a number of factors that have rocketed the reach of this post. I'll go into more detail on these techniques in another book that focuses on improving your content but for now:

- This was a highly newsworthy story of immense relevance to the Musicademy fan base

- The story was about two celebrities, again of high interest to the fan base

- The link I shared was from Huffington Post, a Blue Badge verified Page that is likely classified in the News/Media category of Pages

- Another Page, Fuller Theological Seminary, a reputable Page with about 14,000 fans, was tagged in the post (this Page would also have a reasonable overlap with the Musicademy fan base in terms of interests and profile)
- It pulled a relatively controversial quote from the article
- The title was compelling with a controversial sub heading
- The body copy also asked people if they agreed with the article (encouraging them to engage in an intelligent way)
- It was posted at optimal time for Musicademy's UK and US audience – when most were online
- As soon as it was posted, the story started to get lots of clicks and reactions

All the above are factors that optimise a post for reach.

These additional factors will have further skyrocketed reach:

- There were some 63 reactions (Likes etc)
- There were 31 shares
- There were over 21 comments

All the above will have increased the viral spread of the post so lots of people saw the story who weren't actually fans of the Page. You can get an idea of the proportion of each by going to your Facebook Insights. Select Posts and click the down arrow to select Reach:Fans / Non-Fans.

You can see that about half of this post's reach was to non fans.

All Posts Published

Published ▼	Post	Type	Targeting	Reach	Engagement
04/29/2016 1:26 pm	Here's the performance of a song developed during a recent G			2.5K	31 5
04/28/2016 10:52 am	You'll be seeing plenty in your news feed this week about Bon			11K	1.2K 191
04/26/2016 4:21 pm	The low down from CCLI UK and CCLI TV on copyright in song			1.4K	25 2

For even more specific data go to Insights, select Export and the select Post Data. An Excel download will start. Don't be scared. It's very simple maths.

Highlight the line of the post in question. Note the total organic reach in column J (in this case 11,017). Note the figure in column U "Lifetime Post reach by people who Like your Page" (5,525). Divide 5,525 by 11,017 and multiple by 100. With the example here that gets us exactly 50% organic reach of fans.

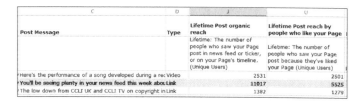

C	D	J	U
Post Message	Type	**Lifetime Post organic reach** Lifetime: The number of people who saw your Page post in news feed or ticker, or on your Page's timeline. (Unique Users)	**Lifetime Post reach by people who like your Page** Lifetime: The number of people who saw your Page post because they've liked your Page (Unique Users)
Here's the performance of a song developed during a rec Video		2531	2501
You'll be seeing plenty in your news feed this week abou Link		11017	5525
The low down from CCLI UK and CCLI TV on copyright in Link		1382	1279

Based on multiple experiments I've done over the past year, I reckon it's virtually impossible to reach more than 50% of your fan base with a purely organic post. This latest little experiment would confirm that.

Don't worry if this is all feeling a bit like you've been thrown in the deep end. We'll back track now and go through many of the key factors that influence the algorithm.

Part 2 – Reach 101: Getting the basics right

Page Categories

We've anecdotal evidence that some Page categories are prioritised over others. When Smart Insights[16] (who we've worked with on a number of occasions) changed their category to Media/News/Publishing they experienced a big and consistent boost in fan numbers.

It's certainly true that some of the Pages in the Media/News/Publishing category on Facebook are some of the most successful on the platform. We know that Facebook is keen to be the place where you discover news. If JFK had died in 2016 you would have found out about it on Facebook. As such it is logical that Facebook will give good reach to news sites.

Verified Pages

It's a logical assumption that Verified Pages rank higher than those that are non-verified. These are Pages that Facebook has confirmed represent legitimate entities – brands, businesses and public figures – rather than spoof or general interest Pages.

Here are three examples of pages that are non-verified, grey tick verified and blue tick verified.

The Digiterati ✓
@TeamDigiterati

Grey tick verified

Mari Smith ✓
@marismith

Blue tick verified

Econsultancy
@Econsultancy

Non-verified

---

16. www.facebook.com/smartinsights

Facebook is keen to present accurate content to its users. Verification is part of ensuring that is the case, reassuring users that a Page has been checked out and represents who it says it is. The Blue Tick is the holy grail of verification and currently generally only available to celebrities and major brands.

Posts from Pages with complete profile information

I really like Search Engine Journal's About information[17]:

PAGE INFO	
Start Date	Founded on June 1, 2003
Short Description	News, interviews and how-to guides from marketing experts around the world.
Company Overview	SEJ is a digital marketing blog updated daily with news and advice on content strategy, paid and organic search, social media, analytics and entrepreneurial life.
Long Description	Search Engine Journal "SEJ" covers the marketing world daily with in-depth subject guides, news reports, argumentative and o... See More
Mission	Helping marketers succeed by producing best-in-industry guides and information while cultivating a positive community
Awards	#10 AdAge Power150 Blog, #11 Technorati Business Blog
Email	editor@searchenginejournal.com
Website	https://www.searchenginejournal.com/

The descriptions are well crafted, succinct and great for SERP (Search Engine Results Pages) too.

Note how quite a lot of information is filled in. If information is missing from this part of a Page profile, ordinary users won't be aware as these fields are absent, but this Page hasn't completed all available fields as you would become aware of in the screen grab below which reveals that address, phone and opening hours information is missing. Facebook prefers it if you complete all the parts of your Page's profile information including all available information fields. Full completion gives Facebook more information to index in search, meaning it is more visible to users. It's reasonable to assume that full completion, ideally

---

17. www.facebook.com/searchenginejournal

with unique content for each field, is one of the 100,000 factors that mean content reaches your users.

What is clear when we look at the home Page for SEJ, however, is that Facebook very much expects some information on their company address, phone number and opening hours – it almost shames the Page into providing this:

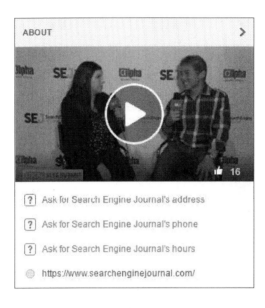

This must be very frustrating for SEJ who likely have very good reasons for excluding this information. For a start, they are more of a virtual company, so addresses and opening hours are somewhat irrelevant. Secondly, they probably don't like to have their phone number easily accessible in the public domain.

On SEJ's website the Contact link is hidden at the bottom of the Page. They state that they are not open to unsolicited guest posts. They do provide a physical mailing address but crucially no phone number and no email address (there's an online contact form).

The size of your Page

The number of fans you have makes a big difference in percentage reach. What is unclear is the degree to which this is algorithm driven or simply the fallout of so many fans gradually interacting less and less with content from big Pages. There will be an element of wanting to "support" smaller Pages, and indeed often a large number of fans of smaller Pages are closely related to the brand itself – staff, friends or family of the people behind the Page.

The evidence we have for these differing reach levels in more recent studies is from Locowise who found that average reach varied from just 2.27% for Pages with 1M+ fans to 22.80% for micro Pages with less than 1,000 fans.

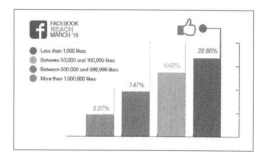

It is also interesting to note the difference in reach by content type between the smallest and larges Pages:

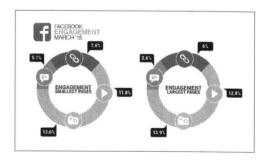

Age of the Page?

In Google's PageRank algorithm, older domains get extra SEO juice than newer websites. We don't know the equivalent impact on Facebook, but it is likely that an older Page, with a good engagement history will do better than a brand new one that Facebook is less sure of.

Are Groups your secret weapon?

Groups are very different from Pages when it comes to reaching an audience. If you are a member of any Facebook Groups you may have observed how you seem to get proportionally more Group updates in your news feed than you do from Pages. That's because the algorithm doesn't really apply to Groups.

When you join a Group, the default is to get notifications until you opt out. Facebook says that this is "Highlights" only but in reality I find it is rare not to see every post.

This makes Groups a far better option for some brands and causes. In many ways they have replaced the internet forums of previous years as in this Infusionsoft User Group example comprised of people using Infusionsoft software. Members post technical questions in the Group and receive an extraordinary amount of free support from other users.

I've even read recently of organisations abandoning the traditional communication workhouse – the email newsletter – in favour of Facebook Groups.

I've written a detailed blog post[18] about my experience of setting up a Group for a niche company and getting a phenomenal response in just a couple of days:

It's not just about the algorithm bypass you get in Groups, the members recognise it as a community so are way more likely to chat, share, create new threads and generally engage. I'm putting an online course together shortly on best practice for Facebook Groups. By the time you read this it may even be out so do check out The Digiterati Academy (www.digiterati-academy.com).

---

18. https://thedigiterati.com/facebook-dead-long-live-facebook/

Part 3 – How to influence your reach by what and how you post

The impact of type of content

As we've already discovered, the type of content is a big influence in deciding what surfaces on your news feed. Your personal content preference is one thing, but Facebook's own weighting on content will also factor.

Here are the different content types

- Plain text update
- Photo / Photo Album
- Link – to a website
- Video (note this refers to a natively uploaded Facebook video. A YouTube or Vimeo video is classified as a Link)
- Live Video – known as "Facebook Live" this streams on the Facebook Page at the time of the recording and is then available until the Page removes it
- Event
- Offer

In the past, photos were considered to have the highest weight (i.e. the highest relevance score of all the different types of content) so Admins would often "game" the algorithm by shoving in a photo for no reason other than to get better reach. Facebook soon got wise to this and started scoring photos lower. It also started to enable users to upload photos of their choice when posting a link story (without the content category changing). Facebook knows that users like images in their news feed and images are particularly effective in illustrating a story.

I'm always hesitant to list content types by weight (reach effectiveness), partly because there are always so many other factors at play but also because it does change from time to time. This relatively recent data from Social Bakers[19] is a good example of how different reach types rank for visibility:

---

19. http://www.socialbakers.com/blog/2367-native-facebook-videos-get-more-reach-than-any-other-type-of-post

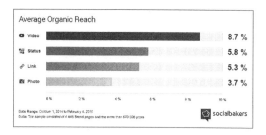

Average Organic Reach

Video	8.7 %
Status	5.8 %
Link	5.3 %
Photo	3.7 %

Date Range: October 1, 2014 to February 4, 2015
Data: The sample consisted of 4 446 Brand pages and the more than 670 000 posts

socialbakers

Video

Right now, (and this was the case for 2015 as well), video is huge. Zuckerberg has been quoted as saying that Facebook's focus in the medium term is on video and Messenger.

I was randomly selected to take part in a Facebook survey in May 2016 that indicated the importance Facebook is continuing to place on video. Here's a screen grab of what was an extensive piece of research into my perceptions of and use of video as an advertiser:

	Completely disagree	Somewhat disagree	Neither agree nor disagree	Somewhat agree	Completely agree
Video content for marketing purposes does not deliver effective results for my business.	✓				
I do not have the budget to create videos for my business.	✓				
I do not have a script or storyline ready that best represents my business.	✓				
I do not have the resources to shoot or film a video for my business.	✓				
I do not have the time to dedicate to creating videos for my business.	✓				
I do not have the resources to edit my video content to make it appropriate for my business.	✓				
Video content for marketing purposes is not a priority for my business.	✓				

What are reasons preventing you from running a video ad on Facebook and/or Instagram? Please rate how much you agree with each of the following statements.

	Completely disagree	Somewhat disagree	Neither agree nor disagree	Somewhat agree	Completely agree
I do not have a video to run as a Facebook and/or Instagram video ad.	✓				
I do not think video ads on Facebook and/or Instagram are as effective as video ads on other platforms like YouTube, Hulu, or Twitter.	✓				
I do not think video ads on Facebook and/or Instagram are as effective as television ads.	✓				
I do not think my video ad is right for Facebook and/or Instagram.	✓				
I have a video I'd like to run as an ad on Facebook and/or Instagram, but I do not have access to the file to upload it.	✓				
The process for creating an video ad campaign on Facebook and/or Instagram is too difficult.	✓				
The process for uploading a video to Facebook and/or Instagram is too difficult.	✓				

It's a good bet that video will continue to be prioritised as it contends with its largest competitor in the social space – YouTube – and also wards off upstarts such as Periscope. So for now video gets a bit of a boost in the algorithm and Facebook Live[20] gets an even bigger boost.

---

20. http://www.socialbakers.com/blog/2367-native-facebook-videos-get-more-reach-than-any-other-type-of-post

We've written extensively on Facebook Live on the Digiterati blog (and we have an online course coming out on it in late 2016). The graphic below neatly shows how consistently good the reach is for Facebook Live content in comparison with other content types. The bar shows reach figures. Those on the left are mainly Live video.

Conquering Organic Reach
Facebook Live vs Other Content Types

Remember that YouTube is not considered video for Facebook (and some recent research we've done would indicate that mere mentions of the word "YouTube" in a post gets reach throttled[21]). YouTube is a massive competitor of Facebook so it's no surprise that Facebook prioritises its own natively uploaded video content. Not only does it give native video a lot more visual real estate on the Page, it also prioritises it for reach.

Photos

We know from the Social Baker's study[22] as well as our own observations that photos don't get great reach on their own. However, we'd encourage you to experiment. One stunning photograph can easily have enough virality to overcome poor

---

21. https://thedigiterati.com/facebook-algorithm-insight-trigger-words/
22. http://www.socialbakers.com/blog/2367-native-facebook-videos-get-more-reach-than-any-other-type-of-post

organic reach (which may well be why a Locowise study[23] rates them more favourably) and it may be that you decide to bypass the algorithm for some stories by choosing to boost a post with little ad budget.

A collection of 2, 3 or 4 photographs cleverly placed images in the collage can generate a lot of traction:

We've also found that uploading Photo Albums (rather than just single shots or groups of photos uploaded at the same time) can result in considerably higher reach figures. People clicking through the images will send a quality signal in terms of time spent. And you can add further photos to the album in due course benefiting from an additional bump of exposure with each new set of uploads featuring on the time line.

23. http://locowise.com/blog/facebook-page-reach-up-by-60-percent-since-november-2015

Encouraging people to tag themselves in photos can also result in better reach as this example from Zappos shows:

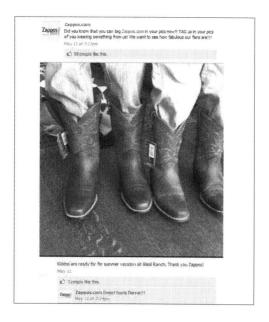

Whilst brands do it all the time (as in the Creamfields example below), it is explicitly against Facebook's Terms for Pages to encourage users to tag inaccurately:

"You must not inaccurately tag content or encourage users to inaccurately tag content (ex: don't encourage people to tag themselves in photos if they aren't in the photo)."

Posts that get lots of likes, reactions, comments and shares

One of the strongest indicators Facebook gets of the quality of the post is the degree of interaction the post receives. If it gets lots of likes, reactions, comments and shares, especially in a relatively short time, the algorithm interprets this as a strong quality signal.

This is likely to trigger a message to the Page admin congratulating them on the post's performance and recommending a boost:

The impact of reactions

What we don't know at the moment is the impact of different reactions on the algorithm.

Does Facebook prioritise posts that cause people to hit the Love reaction over the Angry reaction?

What we do know is that if your users react negatively to a post by hiding it or reporting it will have a negative impact.

Great idea for using Reactions

YNFA have a really creative use of Reactions. They upload a photo with a reaction on that people use to "vote":

The engagement alone from this activity will hugely boost reach. And because there is no text in the update, it's a little algorithm cheat.

Posts that get high engagement very quickly

The first few minutes are crucial in signalling quality to the algorithm. In my experience of posting on a daily basis for multiple Pages for many years, it is absolutely guaranteed that when a post gets a lot of clicks, likes, shares and comments in the first few minutes it is going to get huge reach.

The lesson here is to post at a time when most people are online (you can find this out in your Facebook Insights) and to craft your content for maximum engagement. Also do encourage your staff, friends and relatives to click on the post and if appropriate comment and share it. I'm sure Facebook is well aware of those that do this on a very regular basis but at the very least early reactions indicate to other fans that this post is worth looking at.

Link shares: the credibility of source sites

Link shares can achieve great reach in comparison with other content types. I've found that links to credible source sites, namely news/media/publishing websites or their Facebook Pages do particularly well. There will be two factors at work here. Firstly the algorithm likely favours those credible source sites but secondly, your fans are reassured about the content because of the brand familiarity and perceived trust they already hold for the source.

Targeting posts: audience optimisation

Facebook has gradually increased the level of targeting that organic posts can achieve. In one sense this enables Pages to help the algorithm do its job – by specifically targeting (or excluding) certain groups.

As well as demographic targeting options, you can target by interest too. A new (2016) feature called Audience Optimisation replaces Interest Targeting:

In an age where the algorithm rules supreme it has to make sense for you to target organic posts to those who you know are most interested in the content. Don't use your precious views on people you know the content is not suitable for. Those most interested are the most likely to engage.

You can also restrict the audience to exclude certain people from seeing the post:

You can also learn from the results of that optimisation so that you can better target in future[24]:

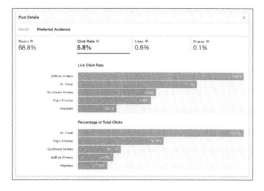

Below is an example of the tagging we do in our weekly Facebook Live Show, Taking the Pulse:

24. https://www.facebook.com/facebookmedia/get-started/audience-optimization

See that we are tagging people interested in some very specific areas. We've found via the audience research tools that our target market are likely to be users of Infusionsoft, or readers of Entrepreneur Magazine. The other tags are pretty self explanatory – leading Pages in our market. It's fine to tag competitors here: no one sees the tags other than you and Facebook – they simply guide the algorithm on who to show the post to.

Tagging other Pages

Facebook positively encourages Pages to tag other Pages when posting. Popping the @ sign before a Page name normally finds the Page. Some Pages have stopped themselves being taggable. This is how that works:

To stop allowing other people or Pages to tag your Page in their photos and videos or mention your Page in their posts and comments:

1. Click **Settings** at the top of your Page

2. From **General**, click **Others Tagging this Page**

3. Click to uncheck the box next to **Allow people and other Pages to tag [Page name]**

4. Click **Save Changes**

It's good for a Page to tag another Page because your content stands a chance of appearing in the news feed of some of their fans. As a Lewis Hamilton fan I frequently see mentions of him by Pages I don't follow in my news feed. Facebook is keen to connect me with other Pages I might be interested in.

Here's an example from a student housing provider tagging a University's Student Union Page.

Pages that the user interacts with on a regular basis

If you are regularly clicking on links, liking, sharing and commenting on a particular Page, Facebook knows you are keen to hear more from it so is likely to surface more of its posts to you. This still won't guarantee that you see everything (unless you go to the bother of selecting "See First" or "Get Notifications") because even your favourite Page sometimes puts out a post that Facebook considers low quality so will throttle reach even amongst diehard fans.

If a user rarely interacts with a Page they will see less and less of its content. The challenge for Pages is to create engaging content that fans can't but help interact with. I'd suggest boosting such content to get it even more visibility in news feed and perhaps re-engage some of your "lost" fans. They liked you for a reason at some point in the past – try to rekindle that interest.

Posts that reference a trending topic

Let's remind ourselves of Facebook's overall mission:

"Facebook's mission is to give people the power to share and make the world more open and connected. People use Facebook to stay connected with friends and family, to discover what's going on in the world, and to share and express what matters to them."

There are plenty of clues in that mission that help us unpack the algorithm. The algorithm helps sort "what matters" to a user from what doesn't.

Discovering what is going on in the world is part of what trending topics is all about.

TRENDING

- **The Handmaid's Tale**: Hulu to Release Series Based on Margaret Atwood's 1985 Novel
- **Mark Farmer**: 'Grange Hill' Actor Dies at Age 53, Reports Say
- **The Human Centipede 2**: Tennessee High School Teacher Suspended for Showing Movie to Class
- **Invictus Games**: British Royals and US 1st Family Appear in Video About Sporting Competition
- **Channing Tatum**: Actor's Wife Gives Him a Horse for His 36th Birthday
- **Paul Lambert**: Blackburn Rovers Manager to Leave at End of Season, Club Announces
- **Thailand**: 6 People Arrested for Allegedly Assaulting British Family on Street, Official Says
- **Dixie Chicks**: Band Begins UK and Ireland Tour Dates in Birmingham
- **Ken Livingstone**: Labour Party Suspends Former London Mayor After Anti-Semitism Discussion
- **Allison Janney**: Actress Who Starred in 'The West Wing' Speaks at White House Press Briefing

---

Trending topics are personalised to the user[25] who can also customise what they see in trending.

Posts that reference trending topics seem to have higher visibility. And they will also get an extra highlight in the news feed reminding the user that this Page is talking about something highly relevant:

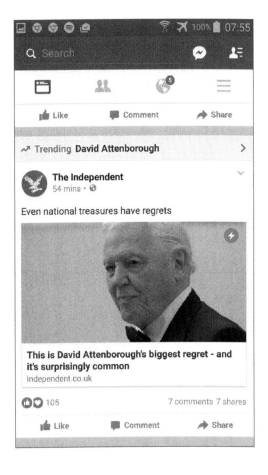

25. https://www.facebook.com/help/737806312958641

Part 4 – Avoiding reach killers

Reach killers: Trigger words

Whilst Facebook has never released a list of words that should be avoided in posts, it is common knowledge that some words affect reach very badly.

Facebook does not like Pages cajoling fans into commenting, liking or sharing posts. It feels salesy and spammy and Facebook got wise some time ago to Pages using the technique to boost reach. We can therefore safely assume that the following trigger words are likely to kill reach:

- Like
- Share
- Comment

Artist and sculptor Claudia Brown was confused why her post below seemed to get far lower reach than other similar posts. I'm sure you can tell why now!

It's very easy to come a cropper by using some of these words unintentionally.

For instance, a link which you introduce saying *"We so enjoyed this article that we wanted to share it with you"*.

Simply re-write the intro without the word "share":

"We really enjoyed this article. What do you think about its take on xxx?"

Now you're aware of it, you'll be horrified by how often you use these trigger words in your posts.

Facebook also dislikes promotional content. So again we can assume that words that are advertising or sales-like will be bad triggers:

- Buy
- Free
- Discount
- Limited time
- Offer
- Sale

You may even find that words like "Exclusive" start alarm bells ringing.

If you really do need to use these words perhaps try popping them into the image – but Facebook dislikes text in images anyway and its antennae for promotional content is so strong you are still likely to end up having to pay for wider reach.

Positive words for improving reach

Although there seems to be little research on this topic, we know from our own personal newsfeeds that birthday greetings, anniversary announcements and generally positive topics get great reach and engagement. For this reason, it's worth experimenting with positive trigger words such as: *"Join us in celebrating our 5th anniversary"* or *"Congratulations to XXX on their engagement"*. Fans like showing support for milestones and celebrations so this kind of wording is likely to encourage many to engage a little more with a like or positive reaction.

In 2012 Buddy Media research[26] found that action keywords such as *"Post," "Comment," "take," "submit," "Like"* or *"tell us"* are the most effective for engagement. I'd take that list with a pinch of salt (it is a little dated and before the algorithm started punishing negative keywords – this is a salutary lesson in critiquing your research sources – is research that old still going to stack up in the light of an ever changing algorithm?) as some are obvious negative trigger words. But experiment and see what works for you.

Clickbait, spam and spammy landing pages

Facebook has quite sophisticated methodology for detecting spammy, clickbait-type posts. Stories with what it describes as "unusual engagement patterns" are instantly suspected. Combine that with a monitor on the number of times a post has been reported or hidden and Facebook is receiving a lot of negative feedback, in the form of spam reports and hides, about the story.

The term 'clickbait' describes posts with sensational headlines that push up engagement but whose content fails to deliver when users actually click through. Facebook is so keen to reduce click bait that it announced a crack down in 2015. It gave this example of click bait that won't be tolerated:

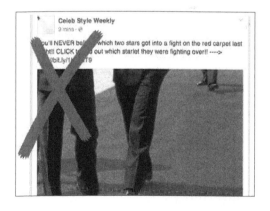

---

26. http://www.socialmediaexaminer.com/improve-facebook-engagement/

You can see how the image and copy combination result in a quick click and then click back once the "answer" to the question is found. Sites such as Buzzfeed saw reach plummet as a result of this crackdown – clickbait is part of their winning formula and they invest heavily in split testing headlines to ensure maximum click through rates on their website.

You often find that Pages posting content like this take people to unsafe or spammy landing pages that are perhaps infected with malware. This is something that Facebook is working to avoid.

Some brands using certain landing page software programmes have ended up being penalised by this crack down. If you're seeing particularly poor reach with link posts to website pages hosted by specialist landing page programmes do bear this in mind.

I'd imagine that on Facebook's radar of identifying promotional content it will be considering ecommerce landing pages from links and factoring those into the classification as promotional and therefore a reach killer.

You won't believe what Facebook has done now... – the death of click bait headlines

In August 2016 Facebook announced further moves to reduce click bait[27]. In a quest for "authentic" stories the platform is cracking down on headlines and link titles that leave out crucial information. The example the announcement gave was as follows:

"When She Looked Under Her Couch Cushions And Saw THIS... I Was SHOCKED!"; "He Put Garlic In His Shoes Before Going To Bed And What Happens Next Is Hard To Believe"; or "The Dog Barked At The Deliveryman And His Reaction Was Priceless."

Facebook had previously adjusted the algorithm to take into account rapid bounces to linked content where the user immediately returned to the platform – posts that encouraged people to click and then return when they found the answer to headlines such as "You'll never guess what happened next".

27. http://newsroom.fb.com/news/2016/08/news-feed-fyi-further-reducing-clickbait-in-feed/

A further step has introduced a system, similar to that used in spam filters, that identifies phrases commonly used in clickbait headlines. Pages or links to domains that consistently post clickbait headlines will appear lower in Newsfeed.

For brands concerned that they might be inadvertently penalised by this system remember to avoid the following two areas:

1. Headlines should not withhold information that is required to understand the content of the article.

2. The headline should not exaggerate and create misleading expectations for the reader.

Memes

The classic meme is a regularly used photograph with humorous text at the top and bottom. Facebook isn't that keen on them (despite users often being very willing to Like and Share them).

As such, the news feed algorithm works against memes. Facebook will use image scanning software to identify the meme and throttle its reach especially from Pages.

As users we continue to see memes because they are so viral in nature. Facebook doesn't ban them or remove them completely (unless they are highly offensive), and the sticky, viral nature of the image does its own work with private users sharing the content.

For brands we'd generally suggest avoiding memes unless they are super relevant to your industry, which arguably is the case with the Glanbia Agribusiness meme above.

Images containing text

Now this is pure speculation on our behalf, but it is based on sound logic.

Facebook has never been keen on ads that contain a lot of text in the image. They look like, well, ads. And no one wants their news feed covered in ads.

As such until mid 2016, there was a strictly enforced limit of 20% text in ad images and despite lifting this restriction, the ads algorithm still reduces the reach of ads that contain a lot of text. It's therefore logical to conclude that the same image sweeping technology that looks for memes will spot text in organic images and factor that into the ranking.

Hoaxes

Facebook hates the viral hoax. And it has often been named in the nature of the hoax itself – people thinking that posting some kind of legal notice on their Profile will protect their copyright and privacy rights. Or Mark Zuckerburg giving away some of his fortune via an online competition that inevitably involves liking and sharing a Page.

Unfortunately, despite people reporting obvious hoaxes there are still a lot of gullible people out there. Sites like Snopes are helpful in identifying suspected hoax posts. There are a couple of examples below:

Neither of these Pages (apparently Qantas and Tiffany) are verified so that is the first clue. And there is a suspicious looking full stop after the Qantas Airline's brand name.

The originators of these hoaxes are dodgy Pages that are being farmed for fans before selling onto even more stupid companies that think that "inheriting" a Page with lots of fans is a good thing. Yes, it might look good for a brand to have hundreds thousands of fans, but it will do your reach no good at all the long run.

Negative feedback

It's easy for users to report or hide your posts, or unfollow your Page. This "negative feedback" affects how your Page is ranked. Occasional negative feedback is commonplace but if it turns into a regular occurrence or represent an unusually high percentage of your content your Page reach will suffer. Keep an eye on it as an overall percentage (you'll need to download your Post data in Insights to do that) and if particular content is triggering it perhaps rethink your content in future.

Content that is new to the Open Graph

One of the reasons Facebook clamps down on memes is that it wants to avoid lots of repetitive content in individual news feeds. As such it often combines stories when multiple Friends and Pages share the same link.

When you use images, videos or links that have already been indexed on the Open Graph, Facebook is aware that the user may already have seen it before. Some images are simply so newsworthy and popular that their fame will rise above any algorithm impact:

But for brands it is important to try and mix the content up. Don't repeat images – not only is the algorithm aware of the repeat, but psychologically the user is already ignoring it because they assume they've seen it before, even if, as with the example below, the written copy is different:

The novelty of your images seems to be important. Stock photography can look familiar to users and won't always perform as well organically as original photographs.

At The Digiterati we've found that keeping to the same corporate look on Facebook videos can even be detrimental. This is likely to be because users think it's something they've seen before, and ignore the post. Here's how our approach to our video guides has evolved to deal with this perceived repetition:

We're now tending to use a totally unique main image rather than the more corporate approach on the left.

Repeated posts

In a similar fashion to the above example, watch out for repeating content in posts. In the example below, Motability Events are enjoying a multi-day event and are posting about it on a daily basis. But instead of showing a great photo of their stand (or even the outside of the building), they've posted the same website link three days running and have somehow repeated a time sensitive post twice:

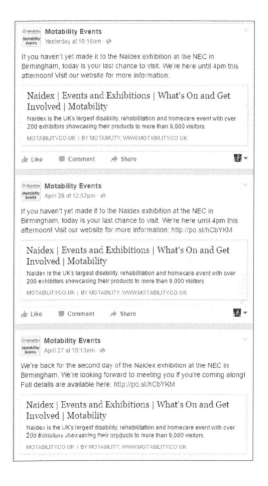

Compare this with Dyson's posts about an event they were exhibiting at:

It was good to see an improvement from Motability in a subsequent post:

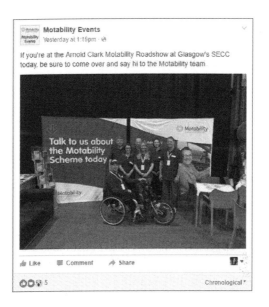

The same organisation had even ventured into timelapse video on a more recent event so great to see their usage of the platform evolving to some cutting edge techniques.

Posts that have the same content as ads

In a similar vein to the repeated content in posts we have already discussed, in our experience the algorithm does not like organic posts that repeat the same images or copy from ads.

We've done a little experimentation on this front ourselves and you can see from the screen grabs below that the left hand organic post is virtually identical to the ad on the right hand side.

If you want to use identical copy and images in an ad, first create the post then boost the post rather than creating a separate ad in addition to the post.

As an aside from this, if you have created an ad that is highly effective, should you use the same ad for a future campaign? I would certainly duplicate into the second campaign but certainly make sure sufficient time has passed since the first if you are targeting an identical audience.

Don't share posts

When you find something on another Facebook Page that you want to share with your fans, don't hit the share button! Based on our (and others) experiments, this doesn't seem to get anything like the reach that you recreating the content and @ tagging the initial Page to give them credit. In the past, the share used to give the original Page a lot of visibility, but that isn't the case anymore anyhow.

Don't post too often

Even brands and individuals that we really love can get a bit wearing when they post too frequently. Facebook is aware of that, and the algorithm will suppress your Page's output if it posts too often.

We've also observed a second and third post of the day apparently killing the reach of the day's first post. So post at decent intervals and get a feel for the optimum frequency of posts for your audience. A news outlet such as a newspaper or the BBC's news channel will be able to post way more regularly than a more regular Page.

Users can become overwhelmed with too much content. And they will easily become bored if that content is repetitive or uninteresting. This will drive engagement down, which in turn will squash your reach.

For both your fans and the algorithm it is best to have one great post on Facebook than many low-engagement posts.

Low engagement posts and pages

Facebook reigns in the reach of posts that get low engagement. And I see those tumbleweed posts and pages all too often when we examine poorly performing Pages. Low engagement from fans is a red flag to Facebook that will lower the overall ranking of the Page.

In the example below there is simply zero engagement in the posts despite a number of questions that are posted. It may be that the Page's Insights actually show amazing reach and engagement (but I doubt it), but the total absence of reactions is just plain embarrassing.

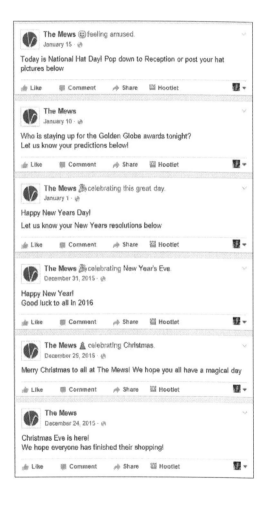

We are working on an online course and ebook aimed at improving your content and avoiding the tumbleweed effect so do keep an eye out for that.

Promotional content

Facebook really dislikes anything it considers to be promotional content. Some content is very obviously promotional such as the Morphy Richards post on the left below that really just looks like an ad and will have had to be boosted to get any traction at all.

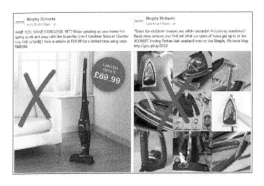

The post to the right is better but in my experience, this would also have been deemed promotional. To be honest I really don't have any issue with Facebook squashing promotional content. If brands are using the platform as an advertising channel for products then they really should pay for that. Boosting a post is not that expensive and considerably cheaper than other advertising methods.

BRITA do promotional content well:

None of the text or images on these BRITA posts are likely to trigger the promotional alarms at Facebook but the brand is clearly getting across messages about filtered water being better and reducing pollution which will be clear strategic positioning for the brand outside of the "sell more filters" objective.

This is what Facebook means when they advise brands doing promotional posts to do so with "context"[28].

Similarly US brand Lowe's does well in a post that would otherwise be seen as an ad for water sprinklers:

---

28. https://www.facebook.com/business/news/update-to-facebook-news-feed

Dyson have a whole series of animated images that are relevant to their efficient household cleaning mission and subtly promote their products.

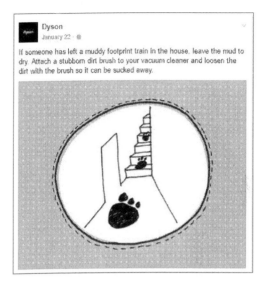

Here's a little experiment I carried out with Musicademy (that's me in the video). The first post was obviously a promotional piece and it got pretty dismal organic reach so I boosted it.

But when I set up a little impromptu Facebook Live video, talking about the same product but using Facebook Live, I earned an organic reach that was about eight times higher than the link post. The novelty factor of using Facebook Live (Facebook's newly launched tool which it is favouring in the algorithm) is helping my reach.

The key takeaway here is to avoid obvious product shots (Dyson do this well with close-ups) and definitely avoid sales-type trigger words.

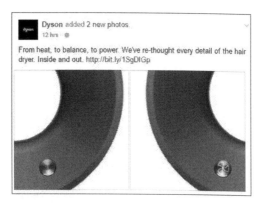

New Facebook features

The only thing consistent about Facebook is the regular changes, updates and new features the site makes. We find that when new features are rolled out, they tend to be given at least a temporary bump in additional news feed visibility. This was the case when Check-ins, Instant Articles and Facebook Live were all introduced.

The lesson here is to jump on the new feature bandwagon early. You'll get good reach and the novelty factor of the new feature will benefit you too.

We did this with Canvas recently (Canvas is a mobile-first ad type that provides a more "immersive" experience but that can also surface as an organic post). The combined effect of novelty and bump in reach achieved some great engagement.

Part 5 – Other factors, tricks and tips

Posts that are Liked or Commented on by a friend

It goes without saying that if a friend shares a post then you are likely to see it (assuming you have relatively close Facebook juice with that friend).

But someone simply commenting on or just liking a post (or Page) will also surface in the news feeds of a lot of their friends. This is what accounts for the viral reach of your posts even when they haven't been shared.

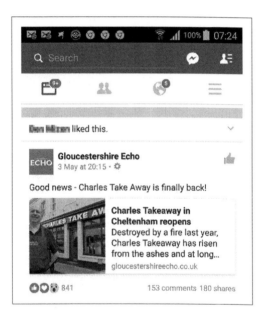

Pages where the fanbase overlaps with that of another Page

Facebook is on the look out for quality signals in relation to your Page and your fan base. It's well aware that some Pages have "bought" fans in the past. Those fake fans will look very different to true fans. One way of Facebook reassuring itself is when your fanbase overlaps with that of another reputable Page. Take the four examples below – they will all have fans sharing common interests, and many of those fans will Like one or more of the other Pages.

How your followers found the Page?

I've deliberately put a question mark at the end of the title of this factor as it's pure speculation on my part. But I'd suggest that of those 100,000+ factors one might be about how your fans found your Page. Let's consider the various journeys that all represent a different degree of keenness to seek your Page or brand out:

- User searches for the Page using Facebook's internal search or guessing at your Facebook @name in the url
- User clicks to the Page from the company website
- User sees and follows an ad for the Page
- User clicks through from another website or Page's post
- User clicks through from a Post from a friend

I'd suggest that the keenest fan is likely to be the person that pro actively sought out the Page via Facebook's internal search.

I'm not sure that there is a lot you can do to influence this other than having great presence and awareness outside of Facebook that might drive people to find you. Facebook prompts on products and "Find us on Facebook" signage will all help (as well as the new messenger codes). But you should already be doing all this!

Posts that get tagged

We've already discussed tagging in the section on photos but it's worth stating that in the context of reactions to posts, a tag is highly likely to send a positive quality message to Facebook. Campbell Property do this well with their student audience:

Content that people spend time on

Facebook has always been aware of how much time your thumb hovers over a certain post or how long you spend watching a video[29] but with the launch of Instant Articles it is also able to track time spent reading articles. People often don't Like or Comment on articles that they read but the time spent on them is an important quality signal.

---

29. http://www.adweek.com/socialtimes/facebook-news-feed-algorithm-change-factoring-in-actions-taken-on-videos

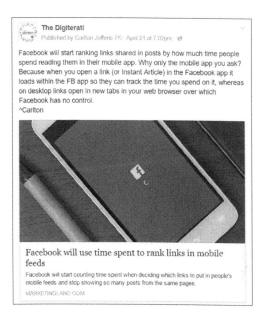

The Digiterati
Published by Carlton Jefferis [?] · April 21 at 7:02pm · ✎

Facebook will start ranking links shared in posts by how much time people spend reading them in their mobile app. Why only the mobile app you ask? Because when you open a link (or Instant Article) in the Facebook app it loads within the FB app so they can track the time you spend on it, whereas on desktop links open in new tabs in your web browser over which Facebook has no control.
^Carlton

Facebook will use time spent to rank links in mobile feeds

Facebook will start counting time spent when deciding which links to put in people's mobile feeds and stop showing so many posts from the same pages.

MARKETINGLAND.COM

Long articles don't just automatically get bumped up here – the algorithm has an allowance to account for the time spent relative to the length of the article, just as it does for view time of videos. Your video Insights data figures show you the percentage of users that have watched a video to completion:

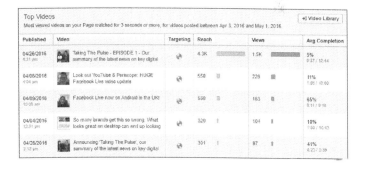

Top Videos
Most viewed videos on your Page watched for 3 seconds or more, for videos posted between Apr 1, 2016 and May 1, 2016.

Published	Video	Targeting	Reach	Views	Avg Completion
04/26/2016 4:31 pm	Taking The Pulse - EPISODE 1 - Our summary of the latest news on key digital	🌐	4.3K	1.5K	5% 0:37 / 12:44
04/08/2016 4:04 pm	Look out YouTube & Periscope: HUGE Facebook Live video update	🌐	550	226	11% 1:06 / 10:00
04/09/2016 10:08 am	Facebook Live now on Android in the UK!	🌐	550	163	65% 0:11 / 0:18
04/04/2016 12:01 pm	So many brands get this so wrong. What looks great on desktop can end up looking	🌐	320	104	10% 1:03 / 10:43
04/26/2016 2:12 pm	Announcing 'Taking The Pulse', our summary of the latest news on key digital	🌐	301	97	41% 0:25 / 0:59

Hashtags

Logic would have it that including a hashtag in your Facebook post would help improve reach – after all that's the way hashtags work on Twitter and Instagram. But a 2013 survey[30] by Edgerank Checker found the opposite to be true. In analysing 35,000 Facebook posts, of which 6,000 contained hashtags, it found that viral reach was actually less on the hashtagged posts.

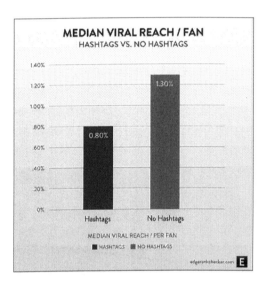

Facebook responded to the survey by saying:

"Pages should not expect to get increased distribution simply by sticking irrelevant hashtags in their posts. The best thing for Pages (that want increased distribution) to do is focus on posting relevant, high quality-content – hashtags or not. Quality, not hashtags, is what our News Feed algorithms look for so that Pages can increase their reach."

---

30. http://phys.org/news/2013-09-viral-hashtags-facebook.html
   (original Edgerank Checker post has been removed)

So what is going on here? Firstly, hashtags are not used on Facebook in the same way as on Twitter and Instagram. On these platforms users are actively searching for content with hashtags of interest (some using IFTTT programs to search and auto retweet such content). Many Facebook users are unaware that clicking on a hashtag will bring up other public mentions. Those that are will often suspect cross posting from Twitter or Instagram.

Secondly, Facebook hashtags will be affected by the privacy settings that most users have in place. If your post is private, no one outside your designated audience will see the content regardless of the hashtag. That means that hashtags that do have visibility are more likely to be from Pages and quite possibly promotional in content as part of an official promotion or competition – something most users probably aren't interested in and we know that promotional content in posts results in squashed reach.

Drive traffic to your Page from other sources

Any interaction with your Page or a specific post is an indicator to Facebook. Use your email list to drive traffic to your Page, perhaps by linking to a post. Embed posts onto your website as we've done below with our Taking The Pulse show:

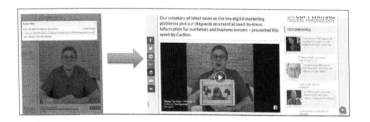

If you run a relevant Facebook Group use that to send traffic – remember that the reach on Group posts is much higher. Here's an example of me sharing a Digiterati Page post on a private Digiterati Group we run. These shares always result in additional clicks and new fans:

Encourage user generated content

Again encourage interaction in creative ways. Get people tagging themselves and others on the Page as we've already discussed.

This Motability post would be a good place to encourage tagging:

If you are running an event, create the event in Facebook and people will tag themselves if they are attending – this surfaces nicely on friend's walls:

Other UGC type ideas include running an hour of Q&A on the timeline – you could do this in multiple threads or via an online "event". Unboxing videos and photos can be really popular, especially if you add an element of reward to it. Photos of unusual uses of the product or the product in far flung destinations?

Part 6 – Other ways of beating the algorithm

Post when your audience is online

I've lost count of the number of posts I've read from so-called experts giving the magic time and day of the week to post. There is no common best time. And even if there was, as soon as a bunch of Pages start posting then, it suddenly becomes the worst time to post.

But it's worth reviewing the research to see what opportunities emerge. In 2015 Buzzsumo researched 500 Million Facebook posts[31] in conjunction with Mari Smith. Mari summed up the research findings as follows:

1. Posts published from 10 – 11 PM EST get 88% more interactions than the average Facebook post. *

2. Image posts get 179% more interactions than the average Facebook post.

3. Posts ending with a question get 162% more interactions than the average post.

4. Videos are the most shared post type, with 89.5 average Facebook Shares. **

5. Posts published on Sunday get 52.9% more interactions than the average Facebook post.

6. Excluding images, posts with 150-200 characters performed the best, averaging 238.75 Shares.

7. Posting with a 3rd party tool results in 89.5% less engagement than directly posting to Facebook.

8. Posts that link to long form content (2000+ words) receive 40% more interactions than linking to short form content.

FOOTNOTE:

* Interactions = Likes + Shares + Comments
** BuzzSumo counted only Shares, not Likes + Comments.

---

31. http://www.marismith.com/8-facebook-engagement-stats-every-marketer-needs-to-know/

The above data explores well beyond simple reach figures, but we know that engagement drives reach, so these factors are indeed worth considering. The extraordinarily high engagement rate for images counters the relatively low reach afforded by the algorithm for that type of post. This means that the engagement is a much higher factor in pushing photo posts up the news feed than the rest of the algorithm.

I would take the optimum time of day findings with a pinch of salt. These may work well for Pages with fans in a single time zone, but for pages serving an international audience the key is in finding a time when the majority of fans are awake. Your Insights data can show you the proportion of fans in each country.

I'd totally agree with the findings in relation to evening and Sunday postings. But my own experience of working with B2B brands on Facebook is that, for them, these timings work less well than the midweek morning and evening commute. So experiment and see what works for your Page. Don't be scared of trying some unusual times.

And do use your Facebook Insights data to inform your experiments.

Here are two very different profiles (from Facebook Insights):

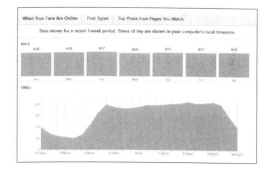

In this first example, the audience is primarily in the UK and it's a B2B company. See how the peak is during the morning and evening commute. These would be good times to post – certainly not between 9am and 1pm. Save it for the lunch break or later in the afternoon.

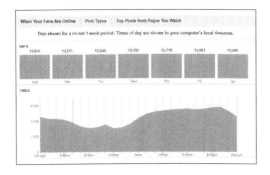

This second example is for a B2C brand that works in English speaking countries across the world but mainly the UK and US. Note how much later in the day the optimum posting time is. You'd want to be posting at around 9pm to this audience.

Remember that you get a window of perhaps up to two hours of average visibility. But do combine that with what we know about the importance of early engagement with a post. Choosing a time at around the peak Facebook viewing hours of your audience is wise.

Posting when the competition is not

Your posts fight for visibility with other Page posts as well as those from Profiles. Many brands post a lot less in the evenings and weekends because their staff, or agency staff, are unavailable to monitor reactions and respond to comments.

This could therefore be a great time for you to experiment with posting.

Scheduling posts

Facebook's scheduling tool is really useful for busy Admins. It enables you to select a date in the future to publish a post:

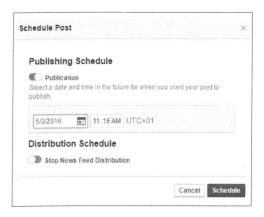

In relation to the impact on reach, it's hard to tell. Logic tells us (with the exception of an embargoed piece) proper news shouldn't be scheduled. It's hot now so why hold back on releasing it. By the time it's live on your Page it may no longer be relevant or has already been seen in another form in other sources.

But of course we know that we need to dance around creating a space amongst other updates as well as posting at optimal times for visibility. Facebook may consider scheduled posts to be less newsworthy. You'll need to experiment with what works for you.

Scheduling using third party tools

In November 2015 Buzzsumo carried out research[32] on 500 million Facebook posts and concluded that use of third party tools such as Buffer or HootSuite over native posting on Facebook does not affect reach. Prior to 2011 this was not the case, something Facebook addressed with an algorithm change[33]. Despite this, the suggestion continues that use of

32. https://blog.bufferapp.com/3rd-party-facebook
33. https://blog.bufferapp.com/facebook-stops-penalizing-third-party-apps-focuses-on-posting-quality

third party tools effects reach. Done properly it does not, but many Admins use such tools for speed and convenience so end up inevitably compromising their content quality. I've seen many recent posts in social media Mastermind Groups from experienced Admins who insist that third party tools do result in decreased reach so do ensure you split test yourself to be sure.

I'd suggest that posting natively also disciplines you to think about the unique options for *that* platform. We all see far too many Twitter-style updates appearing on Facebook thanks to auto posting by third party social media management tools. Automating updates for multiple platforms will also often lead to image compromise with images being used that are not optimised well for Facebook.

It is interesting to note from BuzzSumo's research that the average reach of the posts they were considering were between just 3.2% and 3.8% of audience. More evidence of how poor organic reach is for most Pages.

Which Admin should post

This isn't a question I've ever seen discussed by the Facebook gurus but our own observations on The Digiterati's Page suggest that a post shared by a seasoned Admin that generally gets good reach (i.e. me!) whereas someone who doesn't have much Facebook history as an Admin (i.e. Carlton) seems to regularly get lower reach.

I recognise that there may be other factors at work such as the kind of topics that we tend to post about individually but it does seem to be a pattern for us. (*Since making these observations we continued with Carlton posting regularly and within a few weeks he was enjoying similar reach levels to me. It appears a new Admin simply needs to go through the Facebook trust/pain barrier*).

Test this yourself on your own Page and see if the Admin who is posting makes a difference for you.

Type of device and connectivity

We believe that Facebook tweaks what it shows in news feed depending on your device and also your connectivity. We know this to be the case with Ads (advertisers can choose which device type to show ads on and whether to show only when connected to WIFI).

It's therefore logical to assume that the organic newsfeed is also tweaked depending on your device type. Connection speeds and WIFI availability should also factor in what is shown.

Facebook gives users themselves the opportunity to turn off autoplay on videos (which is a data suck and of particular concern to users in countries such as New Zealand and the US where data is relatively expensive).

Page Admins should be aware of who and where their users are and the type of content that uses data or requires more advanced devices.

User relationships

On a personal news feed basis, family relationships appear to be prioritised – users are able to show their familial relationships (aunt, husband etc) in their profiles. We also find that friends' content is often prioritised over brand content. Facebook started out as a friends and family network – the presence of brands is more recent, and users can get very frustrated by seeing too much branded content.

See First and Get Notifications

Users can choose to override the algorithm for Pages of their choosing by selecting the "See First" option. There is a maximum number of Pages you can do this for which, at the time of writing, is 29.

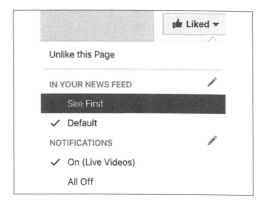

A very recent update to this feature is the ability to select which notifications to receive. Go to the Like button on the Page, select the pencil icon next to NOTIFICATIONS and the screen below appears.

On mobile it looks like this:

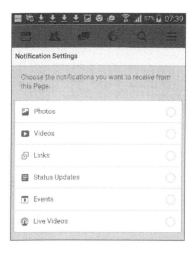

If you feel that your Fans would appreciate a gentle suggestion to select "See First" for your Page then by all means send them an email. For the Notification Settings we'd suggest creating a how-to video or boost a post recommending that they do just that. Here's the video I created for Musicademy:

Non algorithmic factors

The algorithm is not the only thing responsible for why your reach sucks!

Many brands don't help themselves by posting dreadful photos, at a size that renders them mere thumbnails along with terribly constructed headlines. Consider these points to improve your posts:

- **Write great headlines** – the most effective Facebook ad headline is just four words[34]

- **Write great body copy** – research[35] shows that the most effective body copy is just 15 words.

- **Use of additions like square brackets eg [Video]** – the brackets clearly indicate what content type to expect, and have been shown to increase click rates

- **A great image** – a strong, engaging, visually appealing image will promote reach and engagement whether it's a standalone image or part of a link. Photos of people tend to do better. Funny photos even more so. Try to avoid naff stock photography if you can.

- **Correct image size that maximises the space available** – the ideal size on Facebook is 1,200 x 628px. If it's too small it will appear as a cropped thumbnail instead of the full image.

- **Relevance to audience** – your fans aren't going to even skim your post if they don't feel it is relevant for them.

- **Humour** – one research project I did for my Digital Marketing Masters course looked at the impact of humour on posts. I found that without exception, posts that were funny outperformed non funny posts for both reach and engagement.

---

34. http://offers.hubspot.com/successful-facebook-ads
35. http://offers.hubspot.com/successful-facebook-ads

- **Novelty** – the more novel the content (a new concept, information that is new to the user) the more it will get attention.

- **Cuteness** - we're all well aware of the impact of cute kittens doing cute kitteny stuff in our feeds.

- **Shock and controversy** - something shocking or controversial will normally stir your time line up. It will certainly get lots of reactions as keyboard warriors take you to task, which will in turn contribute to your reach. But do be aware of the impact of Hides and Spam reports from such content.

Part 7 – Summary of learning

What does Facebook want Pages to do?

In a little-circulated talk[36] from 2016's F8 conference, Adam Mosseri, VP of Product Management for News Feed, shared some advice on what brands should do to improve news feed prominence. We've covered them all above, and a lot more besides, but this is a useful summary:

- Write compelling headlines

- Avoid promotional content

- Try things – what works for one Page may not work for another and there will be plenty of little tricks and techniques you will discover beyond what I have covered here

- Use Publisher Tools – that's Audience Optimization amongst other things

Here's Mosseri's slide encouraging you to do the above:

My reach is still terrible. What can I do?

Even the most effective brands on Facebook still tend to resort to advertising. This does not mean that you have failed as an organic Facebook marketer. You just recognise the limitations of a "free" platform and use its amazing targeting to push your content out to more people that you know could be interested.

---

36. http://newsroom.fb.com/news/2016/04/news-feed-fyi-from-f8-how-news-feed-works/

A Locowise study[37] of 5,000 Pages in April 2016 found that over 43% of Facebook Pages use advertising which accounted for 32% of their reach.

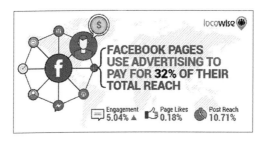

Locowise said *"50 percent more advertisements were served in 2016 than in 2015, and advertisers are now paying 5 percent more than what they used to last year per ad. Facebook has made 33 percent more money per user this year than it did last year".*

Do boost your posts. Boost intelligently with conversion tracking enabled so that you can monitor the results beyond the simple click. Target your boosts to the best possible audience – think about age, gender, geography and interests. Your fans are already warm contacts so don't neglect them. Also experiment with targeting lookalikes of your fanbase – I've found this often outperforms targeting by interest. How about targeting your mailing list (via the custom audience tool) with boosted posts?

There's a whole other book and online course on Facebook ads in the pipeline from The Digiterati but for now you can scoop up a bunch of free advice in relation to ads and targeting over on our website. This is a good place to start:

https://thedigiterati.com/facebook-ad-targeting-overview/

and by filling in the form here:

https://thedigiterati.com/sign-up/

You'll get a bunch of great Facebook resources emailed over to you.

---

37. http://www.adweek.com/socialtimes/facebook-pages-paid-for-31-68-of-total-reach-in-april-report/640316

Thanks for reading

I hope you've found the information here of use and have learnt something new. If you have questions or comments we'd love to hear them.

We particularly like it when questions are in the public domain so other people can chip in, or benefit from the answers.

We have a Facebook Group that this is perfect for – and we'd love you to join whether you have a question or not.

https://www.facebook.com/groups/teamdigiterati

You can also contact us on Messenger here:

https://www.messenger.com/t/TeamDigiterati/

or by scanning the code below, which connects you to us on Facebook Messenger.

What other resources does The Digiterati have to help?

There's a companion online course for this book on optimising Facebook reach where I go into more detail on all the concepts covered, provide additional case studies and ideas for content.

www.digiterati-academy.com

Our website is the best place to go to find what we've currently got available.

www.thedigiterati.com

And of course we'd love to have you follow us on Facebook:

www.facebook.com/teamdigiterati

Other books

We have a number of other practical books coming out throughout 2016 and 2017 in our "Marketing for Business" series.

These include guides on:

- Facebook Live Video
- Facebook Ads Guide
- Facebook Content Ideas and Best Practice
- Snapchat for Business
- Plus a lot more!

The Digiterati Academy

We also have The Digiterati Academy. This features in-depth online courses in multiple aspects of digital and social media marketing. There's even an online course to accompany this book.

Can The Digiterati do some work for me?

As a consultancy we are always delighted to be called in to give hands-on advice whether as part of our social media health-check service:

https://thedigiterati.com/social-media-audit-digital-healthcheck/

or a comprehensive work on your digital strategy.

We're based in the UK but are very used to remote working via Skype, email and screen share.

Printed in Germany
by Amazon Distribution
GmbH, Leipzig